CONTENTS

Brown rocket
green rocket
first I've ever seen rocket
best there's ever been rocket

ZIM ZAM ZOOM!

Rush rocket
roar rocket
zip about some more rocket
let me climb aboard rocket

ZIM ZAM ZOOM!

4

Blast rocket
fast rocket
overtaking Mars rocket
heading for the stars rocket

ZIM ZAM ZOOM!

Red rocket
blue rocket
racing to the moon rocket
won't you come back soon rocket

ZIM ZAM ZOOM!

FIREWORK POEM

Like to be a FIREWORK?

So would I.

To DAZZLE like a flower.
To SIZZLE in the sky.

With a CRACK and a BANG
and a BIM BAM BOOM!

With a WHIZZ and a FIZZ
and a ZIM ZAM ZOOM!

And oh, how I'd SPARKLE
RED, GOLD, BLUE . . .

as everyone below goes

AHHHH and

OOOOH!

7

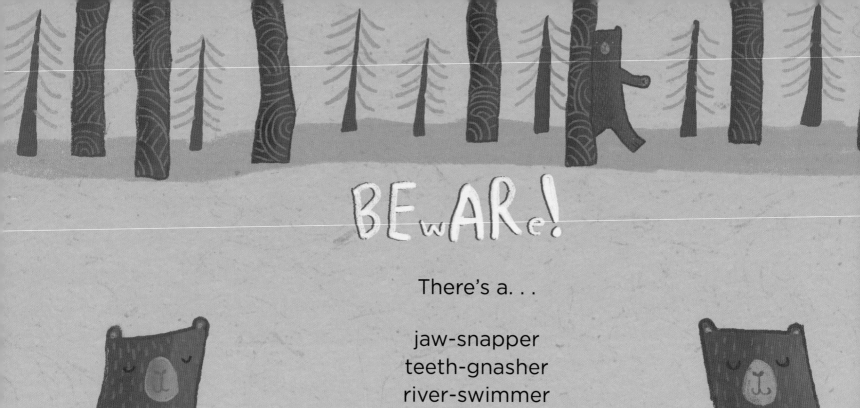

BEwARe!

There's a. . .

jaw-snapper
teeth-gnasher
river-swimmer
dives-for-dinner

fish-catcher
back-scratcher
cave-seeker
winter–sleeper

forest-dweller
grizzly-fella

sneaking, lurking
here and there. . .

you beware –

it's a BEAR!

Lullaby for a Woolly Mammoth

(to the tune of Twinkle, Twinkle...)

Woolly
Mammoth!
Hear me sing.
! Go to sleep, you hairy thing!
! You   can snooze outside my
! door,   just as long as you don't
!!   !!   snore. Come on, Shaggy, shut
!!   your eyes.   Now it's
time for   beddy-byes!

HULLABALOO!

Down at the farm,
oh, what a to-do!

A higgledy-piggledy
hullabaloo!

Listen to this,
it's strange but true.

The cow goes *Meow*.
The mouse goes *Moo*.

The cat goes *Quack*.
The rooster? *Coo*.

The dove flies up,
then from its beak

there comes an *Oink*.
The pig goes *Squeak*.

The farmer? *Woof*.
She cannot speak!

Down at the farm,
oh, what a to-do!

A higgledy-piggledy
hullabaloo!

MISSING: DAISY

Anyone seen my DRAGON?
Scary, Scaly,
Tall 'n Taily
Daisy the Dreadful Dragon!

HAVE YOU SEEN MY DRAGON?
MISSING
DAISY THE DRAGON. SCARY, SCALY
SMELLY, BEASTLY AND MISSED!

She's got bad breath.
A temper true.
Eats old ladies. (Children too.)

She breathes out fire.
She puffs out smoke.
She'll singe your hair. She'll make you choke.

Anyone seen my DRAGON?

She soars about.
She seeks out food.
Makes loud noises. (Mainly rude.)

BUS STOP

Yes, she's grumpy.
Yes, she's smelly.
Big Butt always blocks the telly.

Anyone seen my D R A G O N ?

And she's beastly.
And a pest.
But I love her. (She's the best.)

Please send Daisy
back to me.
Treat her well. Or you'll be tea . . .

Anyone seen my D R A G O N ?

13

Let's Invent a Monster!

Let's give it
a hunk of a trunk.
Let's give it
a stretch of a neck.
A snake of a tongue
a bear of a growl
a bee of a sting
a wolf of a howl.

Let's do it right now. . . *let's invent a* MONSTER!

Let's give it
a heap of a beak.
Let's give it
a hump of a bump.
A whale of a tail
a shark of a jaw
a snail of a shell
a cat of a claw.

Let's give it some more. . . *let's invent a* MONSTER!

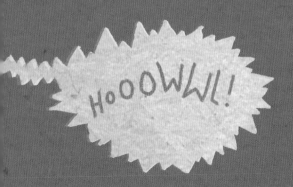

HoOOWWl!

Let's give it
a spine of spikes.
Let's give it
a line of stripes.
And hands and fangs
and horns and fins
and googly eyes
and two great wings.

Then what have we got? The freakiest,
creepiest, beastliest thing.

OH WOW!

IT'S A
MONSTER!

HEY, LET'S GO!

FEE FI
FO FUM

Let's go *once upon a time.*
Let's stroll, let's roll with rhythm 'n rhyme.

Let's dress up in a riding hood.
Let's take that shortcut through the wood.

Let's race that wolf to Granny's door.
Let's huff and puff that house of straw.

Let's trick that witch so cruel, so mean.
Let's swap that cow for magic beans.

Let's climb that beanstalk just for fun.
Let's FEE let's FI let's FO let's FUM.

Let's scrub the cellar, floor and all.
Let's ride that pumpkin to the ball.

Let's drop that slipper on the stair.
Let's clamber up that rope of hair.

Let's sleep upon a tiny pea.
Let's rub a lamp for wishes three.

Let's lick that tasty candy cottage –
break a chair, then eat some porridge,

dash upstairs and rest our head,
in that eency-weency bed.

Bears returning? Let's run faster...
leave them *happily ever after!*

Grump, Grump, Grump!

or... The Three Billy Goats Get Rough Rap

Here's a tale re-jigged, retold,
of three billy goats and one silly troll. . .

The three little goats look over the stream
where the grass grows oh-so-lush and green.
So up to the bridge comes Goat number 1
and Trev the Troll to spoil his fun. . .
Yells Trev, "Oi, Goatie – off you run,
or you might end up in my tum!"

Grump, grump, grump!

Says Goat, "Ooh, Trev – you don't scare me –
cos my bruv's tough, as you'll soon see!"
So Goat number 1 trots off to the grass
as Goat number 2 pops up so fast.
Yells Trev, "Oi, Goatie – off you squeal,
or I'm gonna scoff you as my meal!"

Grump, grump, grump!

Says Goat, "Ooh, Trev – you don't scare me –
cos big bruv's hard, as you'll soon see!"
So Goat number 2 skips off to the grass
as Goat number 3 steps up so fast.
Yells Trev, "Now you just scarper, see,
or curried goat will be my tea!"

Grump, grump, grump!

Says Goat, "Know what, you little titch?
I'm gonna boot you off this bridge!"
Goat came up, looked Trev in the eye.
The troll stepped back and he heaved a sigh –
then leapt in the stream, with a mighty SPLISH!
So the brothers Goat they got their wish.
Gone was Trev, that gruesome frump,
his mean old ways and his. . .

Grump, grump, grump!

The three billy goats had a
well lush lunch –
for all you could hear was. . .

Munch, munch, munch!

Funny Faces

Can you do a *big smile?*
Can you do a *wink?*
Can you do a *little nod?*
Can you do a *blink?*

Can you *shut* **your** *left eye?*
Can you *shut* **your** *right?*
Can you *wiggle* **both your** *ears?*
Can you take a *bite?*

Can you *wrinkle up* **your** *nose?*
Can you *lick* **your** *chin?*
Can you *puff* **your** *cheeks* **up?**
Can you do a *grin?*

Can you *raise* **your** *eyebrows?*
Can you *shake* **your** *hair?*
Can you *make* **a** *whistle?*
Can you do a *stare?*

Can you *pull* **a** *funny face?*
Can you *roll* **your** *tongue?*
Can you do these *one more time?*

Faces **are** *fun!*

Yumtime!

Sponge cake, cup cake
hot cross bun
knickerbocker glory

Yum yum yum!

Red grape, green grape
peach pear plum
watermelon, mango

Yum yum yum!

Pizza, pasta
egg foo yung
veggie biryani

Yum yum yum!

Sometime, lunchtime
feed my tum
suppertime, anytime

Yum yum yum!

21

Splish! Splash! Splosh!

Babies in the bath do it
puddles on the path do it
grannies for a laugh do it

Splish! Splash! Splosh!

Dirty welly boots do it
dainty little shoes do it
drippy doggies too do it

Splish! Splash! Splosh!

Waterfalls and waves do it
giant killer whales do it
little fishes' tails do it

Splish! Splash! Splosh!

Buses rushing past do it
rivers flowing fast do it
raindrops fall at last do it

Splish! Splash! Splosh!

Swimmers in the pool do it
penguins in the zoo do it
dolphins in the blue do it

Splish! Splash! Splosh!

In the summer sun do it
do it as it's fun do it
come on everyone do it

SPLISH!
SPLASH!
SPLOSH!

23

PIRATE PETE

Pirate Pete
had a ship on the sea
had a fish for his tea
had a peg for a knee

    and a tiny little parrot called. . . Polly

Pirate Pete
had a book with a map
had a skull on his cap
had a cat on his lap

    and another little parrot called. . . Dolly

Pirate Pete
had a trunk full of treasure
had a belt made of leather
had a cap with a feather

    and another little parrot called. . . Jolly

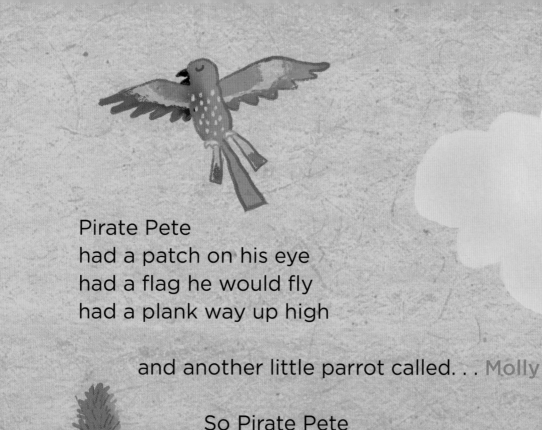

Pirate Pete
had a patch on his eye
had a flag he would fly
had a plank way up high

and another little parrot called. . . Molly

So Pirate Pete
and the parrots four
they sailed the world
from shore to shore –
collecting gold
and gifts galore.

And that's their tale –
there is no more!

25

Have You Met a Wolf?

A white wolf
at night wolf
beneath a moon
so bright wolf
did you have a fright wolf?

Have you met a wolf?

A grey wolf
a stray wolf
half-way through
the day wolf
did you run away wolf?

Have **you** met a wolf?

A brown wolf
a proud wolf
letting out
a growl wolf
did you hear it howwwl wolf?

Have you **met** a wolf?

A green wolf
a lean wolf
looking wild
and mean wolf
was it just a dream wolf?

Have you ever
maybe never
try remember. . .
have you met **a WOLF?**

Teddy Afraid

Does a teddy
take a teddy
up to bed?

Does a teddy
ever shiver
in the shadows
of the night?

Does a teddy
ever wish
that you'd left
on the light?

Does it quiver
does it quake
when it gets
quite late?

Does a teddy
ever wish
that *you*
were awake?

Does a teddy
take a teddy
up to bed?

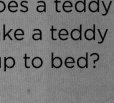

Take a Poem

Why not take a poem
wherever you go?
Pop it in your pocket
nobody will know

Take it to your classroom
stick it on the wall
tell them all about it
read it in the hall

Take it to the bathroom
tuck it up in bed
take the time to learn it
keep it in your head

Take it for a day trip
take it on a train
fold it as a hat
when it starts to rain

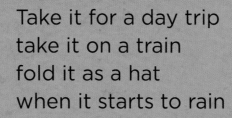

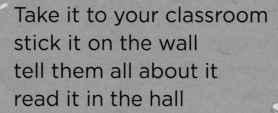

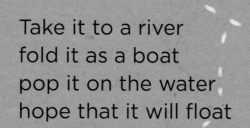

Take it to a river
fold it as a boat
pop it on the water
hope that it will float

Take it to a hilltop
fold it as a plane
throw it up skywards
time and time again

Take it to a mailbox
send it anywhere
out into the world
with
    tender
        loving
            care.

For the Professor of Anthology -
he's one for a pun is my great chum -
Graham Denton - JC
For Gwen - NC

First published in Great Britain and in the USA in 2016 by
Otter-Barry Books
Little Orchard, Burley Gate, Herefordshire, HR1 3QS

A catalogue record for this book is available from the British Library.

ISBN 978-1-91095-954-1

Illustrated with mixed media

Printed in China

1 3 5 7 9 8 6 4 2